WAC GHOSTS, MONSTERS AND LEGENDS

Illustrated by
Scoular Anderson

CORGI BOOKS

Also published by Corgi Books
WAC JOKES
WAC SNAX
WAC ONE-MINUTE MYSTERIES
WIDE AWAKE CLUB: WAC GHOSTS, MONSTERS AND LEGENDS
A CORGI BOOK 0 552 542806

First publication in Great Britain

PRINTING HISTORY
Corgi edition published 1986

This book is set in 14/16 Baskerville

Corgi Books are published by Transworld Publishers Ltd., 61–63 Uxbridge Road, Ealing, London W5 5SA, in Australia by Transworld Publishers (Australia) Pty. Ltd., 15–23 Helles Avenue, Moorebank, NSW 2170, and in New Zealand by Transworld Publishers (N.Z.) Ltd., Cnr. Moselle and Waipareira Avenues, Henderson, Auckland.

Printed and bound in Great Britain by
Cox & Wyman Ltd, Reading

WHERE TO FIND YOUR FAVOURITE GHOST, MONSTER OR LEGEND!

Introduction

Do you ever wake up in the night and feel there's someone or something strange in your room?

Have you ever been to an ancient castle or monument and thought you heard the spirits of the long dead inhabitants whisper in the wind?

When the night is pitch black and there's a raging storm, do you press your nose to the window and imagine you can see strange shaped creatures lurking outside?

You do!

Then here are Ghosts, Monsters and Legends to stimulate your imagination and tingle your nerves. Some are mythical, some magical, and others are based on fact and achievement. There are the Hairy Hands that haunted a stretch of Dartmoor, the heroic exploits of Queen Boudicca, and the more recent reports that gave the Spitfire fighter plane a legendary reputation.

But fact or fantasy – be sure of one thing – you'll stay Wide Awake with these stories!

THE LEGEND OF THE HAIRY HANDS!

After James told this story one sunny Saturday morning – many WAC members were awake for weeks!

Travelling in a car, you might worry about the road being wet, or maybe some patchy fog – but the last thing you'd be looking out for is a pair of huge hairy hands!

But that's what appeared – and several times – on the lonely roads of Dartmoor in Devon.

In June 1921, the doctor from a local prison was riding across the moor on his motor bike, with two children sitting in a sidecar next to him. All of a sudden, the doctor shouted 'There's something wrong. Jump!' The children jumped, and rolled to safety but the doctor was thrown from the motor bike and killed. Police could find no reason why the bike had suddenly swerved off the road.

Two months later, on 26 August, an army officer left a friend's house on his motorbike, to visit some people on the other side of the moor. He returned to the house an hour later – his bike was wrecked, but he had escaped with cuts and bruises. His friend thought he'd just slipped off his bike – but the army officer told an altogether more chilling story!

'You may find this difficult to believe, but something drove me off the road. A pair of huge hairy hands closed over mine. I fought them, but it was no use, they were too strong for me . . . I knew no more until I came to my senses lying on my face on the turf.'

The spot where the army officer saw

the hands was exactly the same place that the prison doctor was mysteriously killed.

Little was heard of the Hairy Hands until three years later. In 1924, a husband and wife were staying at a caravan site on the moor. One night, the woman woke up suddenly to see a huge hairy hand creeping up the window – she knew it was trying to get in. Knowing no other way to stop it, the lady made a sign of the cross. To her relief the hand slowly slipped down the window and disappeared.

Since the nineteen twenties, there've been few sightings of the Hairy Hands – except for one – a friend of mine was driving across the moor in a full moon when suddenly a huge hand appeared by the side of the road. Its thumb was sticking up, and it held a strange sign – M4 MOTORWAY TO LONDON PLEASE.

UNSINKABLE

A Titanic tragedy

On Wednesday, 10 April 1912, crowds gathered on the docks at Southampton to cheer the great liner, the *Titanic*, as it left on its first voyage across the Atlantic. No one knew that, three days later, this 'unsinkable' ship would be remembered for a far more sinister reason.

There was no greater ship than the *Titanic*. Built to carry over three and a half thousand on its first trip, it was so huge, watertight, and safe that one of its officers said, . . . 'the heaviest sea can never wash aboard . . . we may laugh at dirty weather!'

But three days later, that officer was made to eat his words. In the evening of April thirteenth, the ship entered the iceberg zone of the Atlantic, travelling at twenty five miles per hour. The Captain ordered two men to the crows nest - the highest lookout in the ship, and left the bridge to join the passengers. At eleven forty, three gongs sounded – a signal for icebergs ahead. Moments later the proud *Titanic* collided with an iceberg one hundred feet high.

The collision didn't cause a great crash – passengers heard a grinding along the sides, and then silence. But that grinding had ripped open the watertight compartments along the side, allowing water to pour in.

It took forty-five minutes for anyone to notice that the liner was starting to dip at the front, and to realise that the 'unsinkable' was actually sinking!

The order was given to abandon ship, with women and children leaving first. But some wives wouldn't leave their husbands, and they became stranded on the doomed decks. While the lifeboats were being lowered to safety, music began to play on deck. The ship's band had assembled in a corner, and started to play cheerful popular tunes.

As the last lifeboat left, the wireless operator was still to be seen tapping out an SOS signal, and the Captain bellowed his last words to the stranded crew, 'Be British'. On deck, the band played on. Waist high in water, the musicians started playing a solemn hymn, with the doomed passengers and crew joining in. Finally, a great explosion came from the boiler room – the stern rose clear out of the water and the great *Titanic* had sunk with the loss of one thousand five hundred and thirteen lives.

And for seventy three years no one knew where the wreck of the *Titanic* lay. Hundreds of searches have been made by treasure hunters, believing that a great fortune lies in the ship's safes. But finally, in 1986, a French and American scientific team came across a strange hull thirteen thousand feet below the surface. The elusive *Titanic* had been found.

The only question now is whether the liner can be raised again. Some say the wreck is too deep, but others believe that by filling the hull with canvas bags and inflating them, the ship will rise to the surface. But should the unsinkable *Titanic* be refloated and its treasures reclaimed, or should it be left as it is, an underwater tomb for fifteen hundred doomed passengers?

QUEEN BOUDICCA
Or it helps to be blue to be bold

English women were treated pretty badly back in Roman times. After they'd cleaned the hut, they would usually be faced with a wild boar to roast, or the pigsty to muck out. But one woman stood out as a fierce warrior and noble leader – Queen Boudicca.

Boudicca ruled the Iceni tribe of East Anglia after her husband died in 59AD. Although the Romans controlled Britain, each tribe was given land and lent money. The problems started when the Romans decided they wanted their money back!

The Queen refused to repay the Romans, so they laid siege to her tribe, killing villagers and stealing gold and silver. Boudicca escaped to the forest and planned a revenge, which was to become one of the bloodiest wars ever fought on English soil.

Queen Boudicca waited until the legions were away fighting in Wales, then, with a force of thousands, she attacked the Roman town of Colchester – killing twenty thousand.

Word filtered back to London that a fierce woman with wild hair to her hips was moving south, riding a warrior's chariot, with a force of hundreds of thousands of troops, destroying towns on the way. The Roman army in London was small, and Boudicca overran the city, burning the buildings and killing its people.

The Romans were in chaos – if Boudicca won another battle she would cotrol the heart of Britain. She had to be defeated.

As the two enemies lined up for battle, on a site near London's King's Cross station, Boudicca outnumbered the Romans ten to one. In fact, the Britons were so sure of winning that they brought their families to watch!

But Boudicca's army was too confident – they attacked the Roman legions in disorganised mobs. The Romans in turn made barriers with their shields, and shot arrows into the crowds of Britons. Queen Boudicca sent wave after wave of her troops into battle, but slowly they tired, until finally the Roman army advanced in a wedge, killing thousands as they moved forward. By the end of the day eighty thousand Britons had died.

Only four hundred Romans were killed.

Noble Queen Boudicca watched her army being destroyed but escaped death on the battlefield. Hours later, she drove her chariot into the forest and poisoned herself. Soon afterwards, the Romans made peace with the Britons. But, despite Queen Boudicca's defeat, she has become England's most famous woman warrior.

WHO ARRESTED PC GODFREY?

UFO, or a Constable's imagination?

On 28 November 1980 Police Constable Alan Godfrey was called out to round up

some cows that had been spotted roaming around the local housing estate. But after spending the night driving up and down the narrow roads looking for them and not a sight of a single cow he decided to give up. Before coming off duty, however, he decided to make one last trip in his patrol car. All of a sudden a glow appeared on the road ahead. At first he thought it was the No 74 bus, but it was only 5.30 in the morning, and the buses didn't start running until 7.00. As he neared the object, it became obvious that it was something extraordinary. What PC Godfrey saw looked like a spinning top, with windows. It was hovering just above the road surface, rotating. The surrounding trees and hedges were being blown this way and that by the force it was creating and although it had been raining all night, the road underneath the object was perfectly dry.

Alan Godfrey didn't panic – he sat in his car and began to sketch the UFO. Then suddenly he found himself driving his car away from the scene. The sketches had vanished – but try as he might he couldn't remember what had happened to them. He turned his car around and went back to the spot where he had seen the object, but it was now deserted.

Gradually memories of those missing few minutes started coming back to him. He remembered hearing a voice saying, 'You must forget everything you have seen today.'

Nine months after the incident PC Godfrey was hypnotised and remembered under the treatment the full story of what had happened.

He had been taken aboard the UFO and given a medical examination by two distinct types of humanoid creature – one tall, the other small – both ugly. Once he'd been examined he was returned to his car, and told to forget everything that had happened to him.

PC Godfrey wasn't the only one to see the UFO that night. The caretaker of the local school saw an object fitting the description PC Godfrey had given climbing into the sky. Could these really have been visitors from another planet, or were they figments of PC Godfrey's imagination? It's something we'll never know!

PADFOOT, TRASH AND SHUCK

Haunting hounds all!

Everyone knows that ghosts of human beings exist – but what many people don't realise is that ghoulish animals roam about in the wilder parts of Britain. All sorts of strange beasts have been seen – mysterious headless horses, weird wild cats, and even vanishing cows! But some of the most infamous ghostly beasts are the Black Dogs. Descended from wild wolf hounds, the creatures are supposed to be extinct, but they still appear all over the country.

In the North East of England the Padfoot roams around – the size of a donkey and with feet that turn backwards, Lancashire has the Trash – which utters a blood curdling screech before sinking into the ground; and the Shuck of East Anglia – with a single flaming eye – appears on stormy nights and haunts graveyards.

The Black Dog is most common in the West of England, where it roams the barren moors and marshes. A local busman, driving a lonely route across Exmoor, suddenly saw a huge black dog with flaming eyes crossing the road. Desperately, the busman pumped the brakes, but couldn't stop in time. Climbing out of the bus, he looked to see if the dog was still alive – but there was no injured dog or even traces of blood – the hound had simply disappeared into thin air.

The busman's sighting must have been scary, but if he'd known the real reason why Black Dogs appear, he would have frozen with fear, because The Black Dog is supposed to be an omen of death.

For many centuries, local people have

told that if someone sees the demon Black Dog, a death in their family would follow soon. In 1885, a ploughman met a Black Dog every night for eight nights. Two days later his sister died. And earlier this century, a fierce black hound was seen immediately before a savage murder.

Don't worry if your pet dog is black – if he starts getting excited it's only because he wants his dinner. But beware if you're crossing a dark moor and you're confronted by a huge hound with fiery eyes – he may want more than his evening meal!

THE SPITFIRE

The story of the legendary World War 2 fighter

In the late afternoon of March 1936 Test Pilot, Captain 'Mutt' Summers, climbed into the one-man cockpit of prototype K5054. Nervously he strapped himself in and quickly ran through all the routine checks. Within minutes the Rolls Royce Merlin engine spluttered into life, and he was airborne. Summers was thrilled with the feel of the new aircraft – it flew up to speeds of 350 miles per hour and at heights of 5,000 feet. When he eventually landed safely to a cheering crowd of onlookers, he said, 'I don't want anything changed!'

This was the first flight of the Spitfire – a plane that bridged the gap between the old biplane and the modern jet. A plane that was to become a legend in aeronautic history. The Spitfire was produced just in time. As the German leader, Hitler, gathered his troops, so the finishing touches were put to the fighter aircraft. When war did eventually break out in 1939, it was the Spitfire that operated in the front line of the British airforce. But it was in the Battle of Britain that the Spitfire really lived up to its name. With only 800 fighters against the 3,000 German planes, it was this tiny, but fierce aircraft, that was hailed as a major factor in countering the planned German invasion of Britain. And, as if in celebration of this fact, it was the Spitfire that was chosen to carry barrels of beer strapped to its wings to the thirsty troops in Normandy just after the war.

There's no doubt that to the pilots who flew her she held a special kind of magic – described as 'The greatest fighter aircraft of all time' and 'An engineering wonder, as beautiful as any sculpture.'

Built in their heyday for £5,000, they now fetch up to a quarter of a million, as collectors' items. Finding a Spitfire is like finding buried treasure, such is their mystique. There is a legend that half a dozen brand new models, still in their delivery crates, are buried down an Australian mineshaft - and every year people comb the country with metal detectors anxious to locate even a wing of the legendary aeroplane.

1986 saw the Spitfire's 50th birthday. Fourteen still operational aircraft took to the air in celebration and, no doubt, the thoughts of some of the pilots may well have turned to the Spitfire's creator, R. J. Mitchell. Although he witnessed its first flight, he died before he had the chance to fly in her. But, there is little doubt he would have been pleased that his Spitfire is remembered by those who flew her as 'God's gift to pilots', and has taken its place beside Tiger Moth and Concorde in the history of flight.

THE YEAR OF THE RAT!

How the Chinese calendar was born

Long ago, before there were human beings on earth there were only animals. The gods wanted them to live happily together. But instead of being friends the animals fought – each one thinking it was better than the other. Things got worse and worse, until eventually, the Jade Emperor, ruler of all the gods, decided to put an end to it.

'I'll give each creature a year of its own,' he thought. 'In that year it can be more important than any of the others, and I'll decide which creature has which year by having a race.'

The Jade Emperor then ordered his officials to mark out a race track and, when it was ready, invitations were sent to every creature in the world to take part in the race. But only twelve animals came to the starting line: Tiger, Rabbit, Goat, Horse, Monkey, Rooster, Ox, Rat, Dog, Pig, Snake and, finally, Dragon. When they were all ready the Jade Emperor shouted GO and the race began.

First they had to go through a thick forest. The large animals found this difficult. They kept tripping over, or getting tangled in the branches and creepers. The smaller animals found this part easier. Next they came to a rice field, which proved to be easy for the large animals, who galloped across, but the small ones got stuck in the mud and had to struggle. By the time they'd reached the final obstacle, a river, the animals were neck and neck.

The river was the most difficult obstacle of all. It was very wide and very fast. Even Rooster, who had been flying, found it too wide for him. Some of the animals began to fall behind, until eventually only two were in the lead: Ox, who was strong enough to battle the current, and crafty Rat, who had jumped on to Ox's back. As soon as Ox reached the bank, Rat jumped down, and crossed the finishing line first.

Then the Emperor called all the animals around him and said: 'Out of all the creatures in the world, you twelve answered my invitation and ran the race. Even though Rat reached the finishing-line first, there is a prize for everyone and everyone is a winner. Each one of you will have a year of your own. There will be twelve years. The first year will belong to Rat and will be called the year of the Rat. After that, you shall each have one year to rule, the year I name after you. When all twelve years are done the cycle will start again.'

That is the legend of how the Chinese calendar began and how each year got its name.

THE MONEY PIT ON OAK ISLAND

Never leave an empty pit overnight!

On an island off the East coast of Canada legend claims that a fortune in pirates' gold lies buried. For almost two hundred years fortune-hunters have tried to reach the gold which is hidden in what seems to be a bottomless pit.

The first person to come across the treasure trove was sixteen-year-old Daniel McGinnis. One day, while out in his canoe, he came across the uninhabited Oak Island. He began exploring and suddenly found an old ship's tackle block, hanging from a large oak tree. The ground around the tree looked as if someone had been digging there.

Daniel paddled home and returned the next day with two friends. Together they began digging. It was hard work, but eventually they uncovered a shaft and immediately assumed they were on the trail of buried treasure.

Ten foot further down they found a man-made platform. They were sure that they would find the treasure underneath. But all they found was more earth. Doggedly, they continued digging, only to find more platforms every ten feet. Then at ninety feet excitement broke out. They had just gone through the strongest platform yet. Underneath they discovered a flat stone, with some coded markings. The stone was sent to the mainland, and when it had been deciphered the message read: 'Ten feet below, two million pounds are buried.'

Daniel McGinnis and his partners felt sure they were near to success. They went down another ten feet and struck something solid – it sounded like metal.

But it was late in the day and the men decided to rest until daylight.

Early the following morning the expectant partners returned to the 'Money Pit'. But their hopes were shattered when they saw that the whole shaft was full of water. They made numerous other attempts, by digging new shafts, but each time they were forced to give up. Daniel McGinnis died disappointed.

The origins of the treasure are uncertain, but it is thought to have been buried by Captain William Kidd and his band of pirates. Certainly a map of Oak Island was found in his desk and as he was led to the gallows in 1701 he was heard putting a terrible curse on anyone searching for his treasure.

LOCH NESS

Home of a monster – or hoax?

Stories about strange sea monsters in Loch Ness have existed for centuries – but they only became famous earlier this century when a couple on holiday saw an enormous creature 'rolling and plunging in the water'. Their sighting was followed by others – some more extraordinary than others. Two people reported seeing a huge creature lumbering across the road – probably on a pelicasaur crossing!

The first snap of the monster was taken soon afterwards by a doctor. Now it looks like someone doing synchronised swimming, but taken to scale it makes the bit underneath the water about forty feet long!

Since then there have been over three thousand sightings of Nessie – and hundreds of photographs . . . but it's unfortunately easy to fake a Nessie Snap. You could tie some tyres together, then throw in a rock to make a splash, or put some rocks in shallow water and make them look like humps. We thought we could throw Timmy in with his water wings on, then drop a rock on his head to make a splash!

But some people take it more seriously. Thousands of pounds have been spent dropping equipment like time lapse cameras and sonar into the water of the loch. The best picture they have got so far is very fuzzy, showing what might be thought to be a fin. From this scientists have tried to work out what Nessie might look like and it is just possible that Nessie is like a dinosaur called a Plesiosaur. However, now Nessie has been given a new name – *Nessiteras Rhombopteryx,* which means 'ness monster with the diamond fin'.

But despite all the pictures and sightings, no one knows whether the Loch Ness monster really exists.

THE GREAT LEECH OF RIVER VALLEY

Sucker!

Most people have heard of the Loch Ness monster but, according to the

Cherokee Indians, a far more deadly animal lives in the water caves near their home. They call it the Great Leech of River Valley. It all started 200 years ago when a group of Cherokee braves saw a great red object, as large as a house, lying silent and still in the water. As they stopped and watched, the animal began to unroll. Larger and larger it became, until it stretched a mile along the water – a giant, red and white striped leech, glistening in the sun. Then the water began to boil and foam and a great column of white spray was thrown into the air as the monster disappeared from view.

The Cherokees turned and ran. As they did so, an enormous tidal wave swept after them down the valley. Only a few survived to tell the tale. Other travellers along the Indian trail were believed to have been taken unawares by the monster. Their bodies were found days later, swept long distances by the waves, with their noses and big toes eaten off. In time, the Indians began to avoid the trail, refusing to use it because of the Great Leech.

There were some who laughed at the legend. One warrior wanted to prove he was the bravest of all. So he painted his face as if for war and headed towards the river. His whole village followed him at a distance, to see what would happen. As he made his way down the trail he sang:

I'll tie red leech skins
On my legs for garters!
I'll tie red leech skins
On my legs for garters!

but before he'd gone a little way the water began to boil and foam. The head of the giant leech towered above the warrior and swooped to bite off his nose and toes in one terrible movement. Then a great wave swept over the rock and carried him into the river. He was never seen again.

That was the last time any Cherokee went near the water, and the last time that the creature was seen. But the legend claims that the Great Leech is still there. And when the water is clear a large shadow can be seen moving about on the river bed . . .

ALL THE COLOURS IN THIS PAINTING ARE GREY!

A picture with a life of its own

In 1964 Cary McConnaughey and his wife Gibson bought a house in Virginia. The estate had once been part of the vast Haw Branch plantation that had been left to decay. Mrs McConnaughey's grandmother had lived there many years before.

By 1965 the house had been restored and the McConnaugheys moved in. An elderly cousin of Gibson gave the couple a house-warming present, a large portrait of a distant and long dead cousin, Florence Wright. All Gibson's cousin was able to tell her about the portrait was that it had been painted at a summer home belonging to the Wrights in Massachusetts, and that Florence had died suddenly just before it was finished. He added that the portrait was in pastels and beautifully coloured. However, when the picture was uncrated and the glass cleaned, they were disappointed to see that the work was in charcoal, a composition of black, greys and dirty whites instead of the glowing colours they had expected.

Despite their disappointment, they hung the portrait over the library fireplace. A few days later, while Mrs McConnaughey was in the basement, she heard voices coming from the library. Thinking some friends had arrived unannounced, she went up to meet them. But when she entered the library the voices stopped – the room was empty. There was no one else in the house.

A few months later, Cary McConnaughey was sitting in the library reading, when he happened to look up at the picture of Florence Wright, and was amazed to see that part of the painting, a rose standing in a vase, was no longer a muddy grey – it was slowly turning pink. He got up to study it more carefully and saw that not only was the rose changing in colour, but that Florence's hair, which had been charcoal black, was gradually lightening, grey skin was taking on the hue of living flesh and colour was creeping into almost every grey and black tone in the picture.

In the days that followed the colours grew more vivid. From time to time women's voices were heard in the library, but no one was ever seen there. Within a few months the portrait was completely transformed, revealing Florence Wright as a blue-eyed, red haired girl, sitting in a green upholstered chair. Thc vase in the painting had turned a pale jade green with a soft pink rose in it. Even stranger was the fact that once the portrait was complete the McConnaugheys no longer heard the sound of women's voices in the library.

A local clairvoyant developed a theory

that Florence's spirit had been locked in the picture because she had died before it was finished. Somehow she had the power to drain it of all colour if she did not like the place where it hung. To restore the colour, she had enlisted the help of other spirits, and theirs were the mysterious voices heard in the library.

THE MAN IN THE IRON MASK

What was the secret of the prisoner who hid his face?

On a freezing night in November 1703, a masked prisoner in the Bastille returned to his cell after attending Mass. He complained of feeling unwell, took to his bed and died. Within hours steps had been taken to make it look as if he had never existed.

Only a handful of men ever knew the real identity of the man in the iron mask. His face had been covered by the order of King Louis XIV and rumours spread throughout Europe as to who the mysterious prisoner was. One theory claimed he was the illegitimate twin brother of Louis, who resembled the King so much it was dangerous to leave him free; another that Louis himself was illegitimate, and the real king was the man in the mask.

Whoever the prisoner was, there was no doubt he was important. The king and his ministers constantly enquired after his health and welfare, referring to him as 'the prisoner' or 'the ancient prisoner'. His food, clothes and furniture were of good quality and he was allowed his rights as a devout Catholic. He was always under the care of the same governor, Monsieur de Saint Mars, who moved with him from prison to prison. He was forbidden to mix with other prisoners and his gaoler had orders to kill him instantly if he tried to talk about anything other than his immediate needs. His name never appeared on the prison records and was never used.

After his death all the furniture and equipment he had used was burned or melted down, the walls of his cell were scraped and whitewashed, every surface scoured in case he had tried to leave a message. Even floor tiles were taken up and replaced and his clothes and personal possessions were flung into a fire.

The only definite clue as to the identity of the masked prisoner came when someone came across correspondence from the King to Monsieur de Saint Mars about one of the lieutenants in the King's Guard, one Eustache Dauger. A record of his birth exists, but not of his death, and references to him disappear after 1668, about the time the prisoner first appeared. Eustache had always been in trouble and was even thought to have been involved in black magic. Could he have been the Man in the Iron Mask? The truth is still unknown.

LUCIA'S VISION

Our Lady appears to three children in Portugal

Every year, at Christmas time, you are sure to hear the story of the shepherds, who saw a vision of an angel telling them of Christ's birth in Bethlehem. Well, they weren't the only shepherds to have witnessed a vision.

On 13 May 1917, a vision appeared to three shepherd children near the village of Fatima in Portugal. On a cloud that hovered above an oak tree, they saw the shining figure of a woman, whom they described as a 'beautiful lady from Heaven'. The lady told the children to meet her in the same place on the thirteenth day of each month until October.

A month later, about 50 people gathered to see the apparition. Some of them claimed to see a cloud above the tree, but only the children saw the lady herself. A larger crowd assembled the following month, but again the lady was invisible to all but the children.

Well, all this excitement in the village was beginning to cause trouble, especially since many people didn't believe the children's story, and on 13 August the children were arrested by the local police. Two days of questioning failed to make them change their story. On the 19th of the month the lady appeared to them once again, only this time in another village not far from Fatima, and told them that they would see her for the last time on 13 October.

A crowd of 50,000 gathered, on a wet and dismal day, to see the last apparition. This time, the shining lady, again invisible to all but the children, announced her identity. She said she was 'Our Lady of the Rosary' and she told them three 'secrets' about the future.

Then something shocking happened. The rain suddenly stopped and the sun came out. At first it seemed to start spinning and then it began to plunge crazily towards the Earth. The crowd was terrified. After a moment the sun returned to its normal position, and then, twice more repeated the same spectacle. Later, people found that their clothing, which had been soaked in the downpour was quite dry.

The two younger children died two years later from an epidemic of flu, but Lucia, the eldest child, recorded the 'secrets' the lady had told her. The first secret was a vision of hell and the second was thought to be a warning about the second World War. And what about the third secret? Well, just as Lucia had requested, her record of the lady's third secret was not opened until 1950, when it was reportedly read by Pope John XXIII. What the mesage said has never been made public, but according to one account, the Pope told some of those closest to him in the Vatican that what the message revealed almost made him faint with horror.

HAMISH
THE DOG WHO CAME BACK!

A Scottie who wouldn't leave his owner even after death!

Many years ago, in the far north east of Scotland, there lived an old woman called Morag. She lived in a small stone cottage all on its own by the edge of a forest. Ever since her husband had died, twenty years before, Morag's only co-pany was a little white Scottie dog called Hamish. But to Morag, the mischievous white ball of fluff was all the friendship she needed. In the mornings, Hamish would jump on her bed, licking her toes to wake her up – they usually stuck out at the bottom. Then the two of them would go off together on long walks through the forest, with Hamish scampering off into the undergrowth chasing rabbits. In the evenings, the two would sit by a big fire – the little dog curled around Morag's feet like an extra pair of socks.

Then, one day at the beginning of the winter, tragedy struck. It was a cold and stormy evening, with the wind whipping deep snow into drifts around the cottage. Despite the weather, Morag and Hamish went off for their daily walk. All was fine until Hamish disappeared on a rabbit hunt. Morag waited and waited – but the little dog didn't come back. In the end, way after dark, the old woman trudged sadly back to her cottage.

In front of the fire that evening, Morag was in an awful state. The cottage felt so empty – and now there was no one to keep her company. Surely the little dog wouldn't have survived in that terrible cold. Suddenly, Morag felt something brush against her leg – was it the wind? She glanced down – and what she saw took her breath away. Sitting by the fire was a dog. Not Hamish but a dog she had never seen before. It had a kindly face and big brown eyes but its fur glowed strangely yellow, like a light. As soon as Morag saw it, the dog got up, tugged at her skirt, and trotted towards the door. 'Follow me,' it was trying to say. Morag knew she shouldn't go out into that wild night but she put on her thickest shawl and followed the dog as it led her towards the forest.

They walked together for what seemed an age, with the glowing dog showing the way, deeper and deeper into the undergrowth. Morag knew nothing of where she was going or why she should follow. Then the dog suddenly stopped and the reason became apparent. In the gloom Morag could just make out a sodden white ball of fluff trapped in the snow – it was Hamish! He was half frozen, but still just breathing. Morag knelt down and bundled him up in her shawl. She'd found her beloved dog – and he was going to be all right! But when she stood up again and looked for the dog with the mysterious glow – it disappeared.

Morag never found out who the strange dog was - or how it knew where

Hamish was trapped. But, from that day on, she left an extra bowl of meat on the edge of the forest every morning – just to make sure Hamish's mysterious friend would never go hungry.

SEARCH FOR THE DALAI LAMA

No natural explanation here – more a puzzle to be solved

In many countries, when a King or Queen dies then their son or daughter usually inherits the crown and takes over as the ruler – but in the ancient country of Tibet, to the north of India, the search for the ruler's successor used to be far more mysterious.

Since 1371, until recently, Tibet was ruled by a figure called the Dalai Lama. He was seen as the centre of religion in the country and had to have special qualities that no one else possesses. When each Dalai Lama died, an ancient ritual began – a search to find a young child who would be born especially for the job. One of the best known of these searches started in 1933, after the death of the 13th Dalai Lama.

The first clue to finding the new leader was found by putting the dead leader's body in a chair facing south. A few days later, the other leaders – or high lamas – noticed that his head was leaning towards the east and that a large star-shaped moss had grown on the north-east pillar of the shrine that he was in. This was taken to mean that the new leader would be found in the lands to the north-east.

The regent, who was looking after the country during the search, first went to the sacred lake of Lhamoi Latso. There, in the water, he saw the image of a monastery with a jade green and gold roof and a house with turquoise tiles. Immediately, he sent out teams to look for the monastery, in the hope that the special child would be there. Three years later the place was found and the searchers reported excitedly that a young child lived there.

Disguising themselves as travellers, a group of high lamas went to the monastery. Their task was to test the child to see if he was the special one they were looking for. As soon as they arrived, the child ran to them, as if he knew them. Then, looking up, he noticed a necklace that one of the lamas was wearing – it had belonged to the last Dalai Lama. The child reached up and asked to be given it. By this time, the travellers thought they'd found their new leader, but first they put the child through some more tests. Amazingly, he could name each of the disguised travellers and he recognised more necklaces and walking sticks that belonged to the last Dali Lama.

Finally, in 1939 – six years after the death of the last ruler – the child was taken from his home and escorted by fifty people and over three hundred mules to the capital city, where on the fourteenth day of the Iron Dragon, the 14th Dalai Lama was crowned on the Lion Throne.

GUY FAWKES

Gunpowder, treason and plot!

Every year on 5 November we watch fireworks and light bonfires – with a dummy of Guy Fawkes sitting on the top of the bonfire. It seems a bit rough to put him on a bonfire – so what did he do that was so terrible?

Guy Fawkes was born in 1570 – a member of a rich Yorkshire family, who followed the Protestant religion. But as he grew up, Fawkes decided he wanted to follow the Catholic religion. At the time, England was ruled by Protestants. They were suspicious of any Catholic who opposed them, so Guy Fawkes left England to help the Spanish army in the Netherlands, where he became famous for his bravery.

As time went by word filtered back to England about the soldier's exploits and eventually reached a group of Catholics, who were upset at their treatment and especially hated the Protesting King, James I. They decided that Fawkes would be ideal to help them with a secret mission – The Gunpowder Plot.

The plan was simple: They would smuggle thirty-six barrels of gunpowder into the cellars below the Houses of Parliament and blow them up whilst the King and his advisers were meeting there. Guy Fawkes' job was to plant the barrels and light the fuse.

In the first week of November 1605,

Fawkes hauled twenty of the barrels of gunpowder into the cellars and covered them up in coal to hide them. From then it was only a matter of time. The plot was to light the fuse and blow up parliament on 5 November. But on the day before, one of the Gunpowder Gang got scared. He ran to the Government and told them all about the plan.

Guy Fawkes heard that the plot had been foiled, but he was determined to go through with it. So, that evening he went back down to the cellars to put the last of the gunpowder in place. But as he rolled the last barrels into a corner, the King's guards burst in and arrested him. In the following days, Guy Fawkes was tortured terribly until he gave the names of his fellow plotters and soon afterwards the whole gang was rounded up and executed with Fawkes.

Since then people have celebrated the saving of Parliament from the Gunpowder Plot – the fireworks are meant to be the exploding powder – and the Guy on top of the bonfire? Well, that's old Guy Fawkes – the man who nearly blew up the King!

THE LOST DUTCHMAN'S MINE

Man's eternal search for riches leads him deeper and deeper into – what?

fabulous gold strikes, but there are none more intriguing than the story of the Lost Dutchman's Mine. The mine is situated in the 'Superstition Mountains' in Arizona and nobody has successfully traced its exact location since 1890, though many have tried and about twenty have died in the search.

The first people to come across the mine were Apache Indians and they showed it to Spanish monks from Mexico. Inevitably, stories of the rich gold soon leaked out and set men talking and dreaming. Many people made unsuccessful attempts to find the mine, but eventually a Spaniard, Don Miguel Peralta, claimed ownership of it. Peralta's grandson, who was also called Don Miguel, was rescued from a fight by two Germans, Jacob Waltz and Jacob Wieser, and as a reward to them both he shared with them the secret of the mine. But Don Miguel's family had had trouble mining the gold. It was necessary to travel there with an army, or else the Apaches attacked, and in 1871 Don Miguel's father had been killed in a bloody battle with the Indians.

Don Miguel himself did not have the money to finance a large army, so he asked Waltz and Weiser to go with him and a handful of men to raid the gold mined by the Apaches. When they returned they brought $60,000 worth of gold back with them. The plan had been for Don Miguel to receive half the gold, but when the expedition was complete, Waltz and Weiser gave up their share in return for ownership of the mine.

When Waltz and Weiser eventually returned to the mountains they were alone. Using Don Miguel's map to guide them they started working the gold stream. Then came the awful day when Waltz left alone for a while. When Waltz returned his partner had disappeared and all that remained were his blood-soaked shirt and tools, surrounded by Apache arrows. Waltz quickly packed all the gold he could into his bags and rode away.

Weiser had not been killed in the Indian attack, however. He had escaped fatally wounded, and managed to reach a doctor, to whom he gave Don Miguel's map. But the doctor never made use of it and when he died the map could not be found.

Waltz returned to the mountains one more time, travelling alone and when he returned to Phoenix he had with him a small sack of gold. He was almost certainly the last person to visit the mine. He died shortly after his last visit and with him died the secret of its location. Because people in Phoenix thought from his accent that Waltz was from Holland, they called the mine "The Lost Dutchman's Mine".

VAMPIRES!

Umpires with teeth

Stories have been written about vampires for thousands of years – even the ancient Greeks had a go with homeric horrors who sucked blood. But vampires really first made their mark in 1842 with the appearance of *Varney the Vampire* – or *The Feast of Blood*. The book was serialized into 220 episodes, each selling at one penny. Even this success was surpassed by the most famous vampire of all – Dracula – who was created in 1897 by Bram Stoker after a terrible nightmare.

The story starts in Transylvania, where the evil Count Dracula plots to come to England and spread vampirism. After killing the whole crew of the ship which is carrying him, our fangful friend terrorizes London until he is chased back to Transylvania, where he is finally disposed of, getting a stake – that's wood, not sirloin – through his heart.

People really started to get batty about vampires when the first Dracula feature film was released starring Bela Lugosi. From this point, these star studded blood-suckers became a bit of a pain in the neck. Dozens of 'Draccy Dramas' were made, with titles including: *The House That Dripped Blood; You Dance Divinely; Billy The Kid versus Dracula* (where the guns go 'fang' instead of 'bang'!); *Blackula* (with a black actor playing the lead); and *Love at First Bite* (where our blood sucking buddy ships his coffin to New York to get away from Transylvanian 'One Bite Stands'). The one thing you can't fail to notice with all these is that the bloodsuckers are all blokes – but never fear. There was one lady vampire called Carmilla who was very keen on corpuscle cocktails . . .

There haven't been any recent reports of vampires in Britain, you will be relieved to hear. But if you want to take precautions, you should have with you all the necessary bits and pieces. A clove of garlic which you can rub into your skin; a candle (at night); some wild roses and a crucifix are the traditional way to ward off vampires. Armed with these, you should feel safe enough to enjoy a vampire joke!

Q: What's a vampire's favourite tourist spot?

A: *The vampire state building!*

THE GREAT PYRAMID OF GIZA

A roomy tomb!

Of all the great and mysterious buildings that were constructed in ancient times, one stands out amongst the rest – The Great Pyramid of Giza. The pyramid, built over five thousand years ago, stands four hundred and fifty feet high and could fit Westminster Abbey and St Paul's Cathedral within its walls. The great mystery is how the Egyptians managed to build it and why it was built at all.

For centuries, people thought the great pyramid was a huge tomb for King Cheops and just a larger version of the forty other pyramids nearby. It had the same burial chamber and passages. But, when the first explorers broke into its tomb, they found nothing but an empty coffin. No one had broken in before and all the doors were sealed. After the first break in, the pyramid was left untouched until the seventeenth century, when scientists began investigating. If the pyramid wasn't built as a tomb, what was it for?

Some thought it possessed a strange power which enabled people to see into the future. After visiting the tomb, Napoleon was visibly upset and refused to talk about what he'd seen. Later on in his life he confessed that he'd seen what his future would be. That strange power can also sharpen blunt razor blades and make plants grow twice as fast! But most fascinating was the fact that the pyramid had been built to an almost perfect shape. There are over two million stones, each fitted tightly against one another, and its height and base fit exactly with the mathematical theory of Pi – a theory which was officially discovered over three thousand years later. Experts now believe that the pyramid was an ancient centre for mapping the stars and served as a landmark from which the Egyptians worked out the shape of the world.

The existence of the Pyramid of Giza proves that the Ancient Egyptians were a pretty clever lot, but the strange power that seems to be locked into the pyramid remains a mystery that only the Egyptians understood. So, if your Dad's razor blades are worn out, build a little pyramid in your bathroom – it may work wonders!

A BRICK TO SWING THE SCALES OF JUSTICE

Poor brother outwits the rich!

Once upon a time, in a small Russian village, there lived two sworn enemies, two brothers, in fact – one rich, one poor – and because they hated each other so much they lived at opposite ends of the village. One cold winter's night, the poor brother ran out of logs for his stove, but without a horse he couldn't fetch any more wood. In desperation, he went to his rich brother's house to beg the loan of his horse. His brother moaned and groaned but begrudgingly lent him the horse. As he had no harness for the horse, and was too frightened to go back and ask his brother for one, the poor brother attached his sledge to the horse's tail. Before long, though, the sledge got stuck between two trees. The horse panicked to get free from the sledge and tore its tail off in the confusion.

The rich brother was furious when he found out what had happened to his poor horse. He cursed the poor brother for not taking more care of it and in his anger he informed the Judge who summoned them both to court.

On their way to court, as they were crossing a bridge, the poor brother was so wrapped up in his thoughts and worries, that he didn't look where he was going and he toppled over the bridge. On the iced up river below, a merchant and his ailing father were making their way on a sleigh to the doctor's. The poor brother landed like a rock on the old father and killed him outright. The merchant was so upset that he joined the rich brother on his way to court to state his own grievance against the poor brother.

As you can imagine, the poor brother was very depressed. What chance had he of defeating his rich brother and a merchant in court? In this mood, he picked up a rock from the ground and thought, 'I might as well be hung for a sheep as for a lamb. I will kill the judge if he finds me guilty.' He quickly put the rock into his pocket.

When the two cases were heard, the judge became distracted by the weight in the poor man's coat and by his continual whispering, 'Judge true, Judge true. I've something in my coat for you.'

Aha,' thought the judge, 'he's trying to bribe me with a sack of gold.' His greed soon got the better of him and he let the poor man off, only telling him that he must give the horse back to his rich brother when the tail grew back. To the merchant he said that he could jump off the same bridge and try and kill the poor brother in revenge for his father's death. Well the merchant was too cowardly to do this – he feared the jump might kill him – and so he paid the poor brother 200 roubles to forget about it. The poor brother got another 100 roubles out of court from his rich brother who wanted his horse back there and then.

As the poor brother was about to leave the court with all his money, the judge came out and said eagerly, 'Now give me what you promised me.' He was very surprised when the poor brother produced the rock from his pocket and he was very relieved when he learnt how close he had been to death.

'If you had not judged true,' said the poor brother, 'you would have received this rock on your head.'

And with that he went off singing and rattling his money bag and no one has seen him anywhere near the village since.

CAPTAIN BLOOD

A tricky time in the Tower of London

This is the legend of the notorious Captain Blood – the man who nearly got away with stealing the Crown Jewels from the Tower of London. Despite being caught, he undoubtedly was one of the luckiest men of his day because he got away with his life!

It was in the year 1671 that Captain Blood hit upon the idea of stealing the Royal gems. He was destitute and penniless, having once been a Captain in Cromwell's Army, and given acres of land, he had been forced by the new King, Charles II, to hand over all of his posessions as punishment.

The treasures were kept in Martin Tower, and the keeper was an old man in his seventies. Captain Blood, disguised as a vicar, appeared at the door with his 'wife', another member of the gang. The 'woman' pretended to be ill, and the keeper looked after her, while Blood cased the joint.

The next time Blood went to visit, he took with him another crook, calling him his 'nephew'. On the wall he saw a set of pistols, which were there for the old keeper to guard the jewels with. Captain Blood managed to get the keeper to sell them to his 'nephew', for a handsome price. The robber's plan was now well under way, and he was ready for the final stage.

The last time he visited the keeper, as soon as the door was open, he covered him in a cloak, and knocked him over the head. Despite his age, the keeper still struggled and was cruelly stabbed in the stomach for his pains.

Legend has it that one of the robbers,

named Parrot, stuffed the royal Orb down his breeches, while Blood had to bend the Crown to get it under his cloak. Captain Blood began to file the Sceptre in two, when one of those strange coincidences of history happened. The keeper's son, who was meant to be fighting in France decided to come home and disturbed the gang. They all ran in different directions, when the old man, wounded but not dead, shouted, 'Treason, murder, the Crown is stolen!' Despite their head start, all of the gang were captured, and Captain Blood, who killed a guard in the fight, was taken last of all.

The penalty for this robbery and violence was death, but something happened which is still unexplained to this day. Blood was summoned from his prison cell to see none other than King Charles himself, whereupon Blood gave the King his personal history. The King gave him a pardon, returned his lands, and granted him a pension of £500 a year. Some say that it was because Blood had told Charles that his death would be avenged by others, and that the King was afraid for his own life. Others that Charles secretly admired this daring man. But the real truth is – we will never know. All we can say for sure is that Captain Blood was the luckiest man of his day. The Crown Jewels were mended and restored.

AN APPLE FOR A KING

Some have got what it takes and others haven't!

There was once a woman with three daughters. Two were ugly and looked like their mother, but the youngest, Christine, was very beautiful. The mother hated Christine because of her beauty and made her work as a servant, waiting upon her two sisters.

One day, Christine was taking the geese to market when she saw a small red hat with a silver bell hanging on a tree. Wondering how it had come to be there she picked it up and went on her way. But she hadn't gone far when she heard a voice calling, 'Christine, Christine.'

Turning round she found a little man, with a beard.

'May I have my hat back please?' he asked.

Christine looked at the hat – it was very pretty – maybe he would give her something in return for it. The little man offered her money, but Christine was not interested in wealth, perhaps he had something else? Out of his pocket he pulled a piece of coal, no bigger than an apple.

'Plant this,' he said, 'it's from the Tree of Contentment. It will grow and bear an apple. Everyone who sees the apple will want it, but only you can pick it and it will provide you with all the food, warmth and happiness you need.'

Christine planted the coal and the next day she woke to find an amazing tree outside her window and, sure enough, there was the apple. She went to pick it and another grew in its place immediately. When her sisters came out they wanted the apple too, but try as they might they couldn't reach it. Christine's mother tried as well, but failed. Christine was the only one able to pick it.

One day the King rode by. He saw the apple and wanted it, and so sent a servant to enquire as to who owned it. Christine's mother claimed she did, and sold it to the King for a pot of gold. But, try as he might, the King could not pick the apple. He was so desperate for it that he promised to marry whoever could pick it for him. So Christine's mother made her pluck the apple. She then gave it to the eldest daughter and sent her off to the King. But by the time she arrived at the palace the apple was old and shrivelled. Next, the mother sent her second daughter, but the same thing happened.

Finally, Christine took the apple to the King herself. It remained golden all the way to the palace. And when he'd taken a bite of it the King turned to look at the girl who'd brought it to him and found the most beautiful girl he'd ever seen, so they were married and lived happily ever after.

ZEBRA CROSSING

An animal's road to safety

Many years ago, along the great Eastern shores of Africa, in a land now known as

Kenya, there lived a herd of zebras. Legend has it that in those days there were two kinds of zebra – white ones and black ones.

The black zebras thought that they were the best possible colour in the whole world, and were much better than the white ones, while the whites loved being white and thought the black zebras were simply inferior.

Both groups, however, shared one thing in common – they were hunted by man and beast alike, and because their colours were so distinctive, they were easy targets.

After a few years, the zebras realised that unless something was done, they would soon become extinct. So, they called together an urgent meeting of the whole community of zebras.

'My friends,' explained the chief zebra, 'we are being killed off in our hundreds – what is the solution to our problems?'

'Why don't we run away to the mountains and hide?' asked a black zebra.

'Because wherever we go we stand out a mile – we don't blend in with the other animals.'

'I've an idea,' said another white zebra, 'whenever I stand quite still in the shade of a tree, and the dark shadows falls on me, I'm awfully hard to see.'

The proud whites didn't really want to spoil their coats with black, while the proud blacks felt the same way about whites. But since no-one had a better plan, each zebra paired up with its opposite colour, and swapped half its colour. And from that day on, zebras avoided the hunters and wild beasts, lived together in peace and equality, and always wore their stripes wherever they went.

CAULDRON OR CREATURE?

A Japanese walking cookpot!

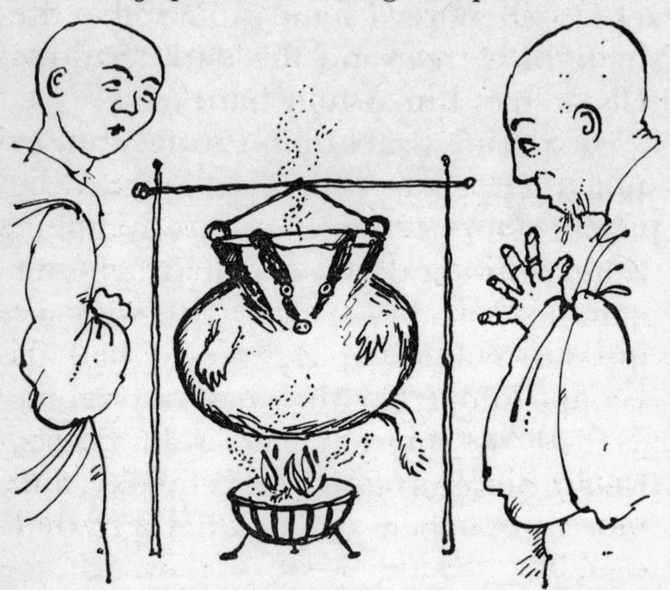

A long time ago, in the temple of Morinji, in Japan, lived an old abbot who was very fond of collecting interesting items, even if they looked old and rusty. One of his favourite possessions was a black cauldron.

One day he called his little priestlings into his room for tea. They made a fire, and put the old cauldron full of water over it to boil. Soon the water began to sizzle but suddenly something strange started to happen to the outside of the cauldron. A little fuzzy head, bushy tail. and four paws started to appear.

'Ouch! Ouch!' it said, 'Excuse me, honourable abbot, I feel too hot. This fire is dreadful! I'm burning.'

The abbot and his priestlings jumped up in surprise – the cauldron had become a little badger! (In Japan badgers are traditionally believed to be mischievous animals, which can turn themselves into different forms to trick people.) The badger jumped out of the fire, and the priests chased him round the room, until finally they caught him, and he once more became a cauldron. The priests couldn't decide what to do. If the strange creature was an evil spirit, it couldn't stay in the temple.

Just then, they heard a rag-and-bone man outside the window. Here was the answer to their problem – they would sell the cauldron to him. The man was poor and honest. He bought the cauldron and returned home. That night, he woke up suddenly and heard a voice beside him. It was the cauldron-badger.

'Don't be frightened, I will not be naughty. I will be lucky for you, and help you make a fortune if you look after me. I had to turn myself into this form to escape from some cruel boys who wanted to ill-treat me.'

The poor man could scarcely believe it, but he thanked the badger, and the next day he followed the badger's instructions to set up a show, where the badger would be the main attraction. Every day the show made a lot of money and the old man became very rich. Then after one of the shows the badger disappeared, leaving the old man alone with just a cold iron cauldron. The man was not greedy, and he remembered the priest who had been so fond of the cauldron. So he polished it up, and carried it with great care back to the temple of Morinji.

He gave the cauldron to the abbot with half of the money he had earned, and there it remains to this day.

But because it is a treasure it rests on a thick purple cushion and people gaze upon it with respect.

MURDER IN THE MAID'S BEDROOM

Ghosts in a smuggler's inn!

In Devon, there's an old pub called the Smuggler's Inn which is reported to be haunted. Early in the 1960s a barmaid who lived in the pub began to sleep badly at night. Again and again she would wake up and have the feeling that she was not alone. No one would take her seriously when she complained about the odd happenings. Then, one night, she awoke to a noise. There was definitely someone in her room. As her eyes became accustomed to the darkness, she was able to make out two figures bending over a third. Then, suddenly, she realised she was witnessing a murder. She began to scream. The landlord came running but when he switched on her bedroom light there was no one there.

That was the last time anyone slept in the barmaid's room. But, not long after, the landlord was at an auction. By chance, a couple of prints of his pub came up for sale. Thinking they would be of historical value he bought them. It was only on his return home that he discovered one of the prints depicted a murder. And by comparing the room in the picture with the barmaid's bedroom it was discovered they were the same.

No one was ever sure who it was that had been murdered, but no one dared sleep in the haunted room again.

THE LEGEND OF ICARUS

Wings towards the sun

One of the most famous Greek legends tells the story of Daedalus, who planned an outstanding and daring escape and lost his son, Icarus, in a tragic way.

Daedalus was very famous for his clever inventions and sculptures but unfortunately had fallen foul of King Minos, the ruler of Crete. Daedalus had no option but to try to escape with his young son. But Minos, as king, controlled most of the important things in life – the land and the ocean. Daedalus had to discover a way of escaping the domination of Minos.

Being a brilliant inventor, Daedalus soon hit upon an amazing plan. Minos did not control the air and if Daedalus could construct something that would make him fly, he would be able to escape. He gathered hundreds of birds' feathers together and, in his workshop, began to make huge wings. He constructed two pairs; one for himself and one for his son and, having finished the frames, stuck the feathers on with wax.

Icarus, very excited at the prospect of flying in the air, put them on at once, and began flapping around. As his father strapped on his own pair of wings, he cautioned Icarus, 'I warn you, you must be careful to fly at a sensible height. If you fly too high, you will scorch your feathers – too low, and the sea will wet them, and you will fall.'

So father and son set off, on their way to freedom. However Icarus was having so much fun that he soared in ever higher circles, towards the sun. Ignoring his father's cries, he kept on climbing higher and higher until disaster struck!

Just as Daedalus predicted, the sun softened the sweet-smelling wax, the feathers loosened and fell from the frame of the wings and Icarus tumbled from high in the sky, into the sea. His father shouted for his son, but could not see him, as Icarus had drowned.

Legend has it that when Icarus's body washed up on the shore, his father set him to rest in a tomb and the island was named after him. It is also said that this legend had such a strong effect on the hearts of the people who heard it that many never attempted to invent any method of travel by air even in painting, preferring to use the tried and tested methods of ships and animal-drawn carriages!

TOP DOG ON TOP CLIFF!

A story of canine courage

A few years ago, a young boy called Jim went to stay on his uncle's farm on the coast of Aberdeenshire, taking with him his Labrador Ben. They had wonderful walks along the rocky coast, but there was one spot in particular that Jim loved. A huge, soaring cliff which, from the landward side, seemed to be a steep but pleasant hill – but from sea was a vertical wall of jagged rock. Jim would walk up the hill from his uncle's farm and sit as close as he dared to the edge. But Ben would never come with him. He would sit yards away down the hill, whimpering and pleading with his master to come back from the edge.

Jim asked his uncle why the dog should be scared of the cliff.

'There's not a dog in the country that can go near Top Cliff – and I'll tell you why. When I was a lad, my father had a dog named Patch – the best dog in the country. Devoted to his sheep and devoted to his master, he was. Then, one terrible morning, Patch and my father were herding the sheep on the hill by Top Cliff and – it may have been the fog or wind, or the smell of a hunting fox – Patch let the sheep stray too close to the edge, and they tumbled over. The whole flock lay dead on the beach below. Patch stood for a moment on the cliff edge, and then before my father could reach him, he threw himself off after the flock. It was said that Patch had gone to look after his sheep in the afterlife and ever since that dreadful day, no dog will go near Top Cliff.'

Jim was scared by the story, and didn't want to upset his own dog Ben, so they both avoided the cliff for the rest of the holiday. But then, on the last night of his stay, he was woken by Ben scratching on the door and whimpering. Jim opened the door, and before he could stop him Ben ran away into the night. Jim ran after him across the farmyard and up to the field below Top Cliff. There, he just stopped and stared. Ahead of him, galloping up the hill, were his uncle's herd of prize cattle – heading towards the edge of the cliff. At first, Jim couldn't see Ben, but then he caught sight of the golden dog, rushing through the herd until he stood at the far edge of the cliff, barking a warning to the cattle. Slowly, the cows turned away from the cliff and walked back towards the farm. Jim's uncle, woken by the barking, met Jim by the yard gate.

'Jim,' he said. 'that dog of yours is the bravest I've ever seen. He's saved my herd and my fortune – and I'll tell you something – Patch would have been proud of him.'

THE SUN, THE MOON AND THE KUTENAI INDIANS

The sun is finally in its heaven

The people of Kutenai, a North American Indian tribe have a legend about the sun, which goes back to a time when the world was dark and cold, with no daylight. All animals gathered together around the Chief of the Indians to decide who would be the sun.

The first animal to try was a black raven. He flew up into the sky, but he was too black and everything remained dark. Next the chicken-hawk tried. But the chicken-hawk was too bright and beautiful, and made the rest of the weather look bad. Then a red woodpecker had a go, but when he was in the sky the whole world looked red.

Since none of the birds were any good at being the sun, the animals tried. First the cunning cayote. He was hot-headed and a gossip. While he was in the sky he watched everything and at night told tales and spread rumours. While he was the sun, the day was too hot – even in the shade the temperature was high, and the river was like a hot bath.

The Chief was beginning to despair. No one was any good at being the sun – they were all too hot, too dark or too red and it looked as if the world would have to stay dark. But then the two lynx brothers volunteered. The elder one was bigger, so had first go. Up into the sky he went, while the rest of the animals watched and waited. In the morning the air was cool and at lunchtime it was hot, but the shade and water were still cool. That night the Chief told the lynx he could be the sun.

But the coyote was jealous. The next day, he took a bow and arrow and aimed it at the sun to kill the lynx. Luckily the lynx saw him in time and directed his heat on the arrow. It began to burn, and very quickly the flames spread. The coyote began to flee the flames, but they sped after him, until he came to a path. Here he lay down. The fire raged on either side of the path, but the coyote was safe until the fire had burned itself out.

From that time on, people have always known that they should find a path to lie down on when there is a forest fire. The lynx stayed as the sun, and his younger brother became the moon, so that there should be some light both during the day and at night.

IDLE JACK

A boy who could have done with a cart!

There once was a boy named Jack, who lived with his mother. They were very poor, so Jack was forced to go out to work. Unfortunately, Jack was a lazy lad and didn't like to have to think, let alone work! On his first day working, he hired himself out to a farmer, who paid him a penny at the end of the day. Jack had never had a penny before and on his way home he played with it, throwing it up into the air and catching it. Until eventually, the inevitable happened – he missed it and the penny fell into a brook.

When he got home his mother scolded him.

'You stupid idiot – you should have put the penny in your pocket.'

Jack was sorry, and promised that next time he would.

The following day, Jack hired himself to a cowkeeper. At the end of the day, he was given a jar of milk as payment. Remembering his mother's words, Jack put the jar in his pocket and set off home. But by the time he'd arrived, all the milk was spilt.

'Why don't you think?' cried his mother. 'You should have carried the milk on your head!'

'Next time I will,' said Jack.

His next job was again with a farmer, who paid him with a large cream cheese. Following his mother's instructions Jack placed the cheese on his head and started for home. It was a hot day and the cheese began to melt. By the time Jack got home, all that was left was a sticky mess in his hair.

'Oh, you idiot!' cried his mother. 'You should have carried the cheese in your hands!'

The next day, Jack worked for a baker who would give him nothing but a cat. It was a good tom cat that would keep away mice and rats. Jack remembered his mother's word and carried the cat in his arms but it scratched and fought and eventually he had to let it go.

His mother was fast losing patience.

'You must think,' she told him. 'You should have tied string around the cat and led him home.'

The following day was Friday and Jack worked for a butcher. At the end of the day he was given a lovely leg of mutton – perfect for Sunday lunch. Jack did exactly as his mother had told him. He tied a string around the mutton and then dragged it home. By the time he arrived, the meat was filthy and completely inedible. Jack's mother was furious about the waste and they had to eat cabbage for lunch.

'Why didn't you carry the mutton on your shoulders?' she asked.

On Monday Jack set off to work for a cattlekeeper who gave him a donkey at the end of the day. With a lot of effort,

Jack hoisted the heavy donkey on to his shoulders and began to struggle home.

On his way, Jack had to pass the house of a man who had a daughter, who always seemed to be sad. No-one had ever seen her smile. She was very beautiful and her father had promised that anyone who could make her laugh could marry her and inherit her fortune. It just happened that she was watching from the window as Jack shuffled by with the donkey on his shoulders and the sight was so outrageous that she began to laugh. She laughed and laughed until the tears ran down her cheeks, and her father rushed out to see what was happening. He kept his promise, Jack married the girl, his mother went to live with them and they all lived happily ever after.

THE GHOSTS OF GLAMIS CASTLE

This will put lumps in your porridge

Glamis castle in Scotland is famous as the birthplace of Queen Elizabeth the Queen Mother - but it is also thought to be one of the most haunted places on earth. In 1372 the castle and title of Lord Glamis was given to the Lyon family, who, at that time, lived in a great mansion in a place called Forteviot. One of the most prized possessions of the house was a beautiful silver chalice. It was thought to hold magical properties and tradition held that if the cup were removed from its rightful place a curse would fall on the family.

When Sir John Lyon packed up his things to move to his new home, he could not bear to part with the cup and, despite the warning, he took it with him. Soon, dreadful things started happening. Sir John himself was killed in a duel. Not long after, Lady Glamis was burned at the stake as a witch – a charge that was certainly untrue. Her ghost takes the form of a Grey Lady pacing the castle corridors. But the curse of the silver chalice did not stop there. John Lyon's younger brother, Patrick, then took over the castle. A wild partygiver and gambler, he was soon to get his comeuppance.

Patrick and his friend the Earl of Crawford were playing cards together late one Saturday night. In those days, it was against the law to play cards on Sunday, and a servant came in to remind them that midnight was fast approaching. Patrick was not used to being told what to do and he rose from the table in fury – challenging the Devil himself to a game of cards if that was what it needed to continue his fun. The minutes ticked by. Then the clock struck midnight. There was a clap of thunder, the house shook, and Patrick and the Earl found themselves face to face with the Devil. He had come to play cards, but the stakes he set were very high – Patrick had been doomed to play until the end of time.

Patrick's ghost is still occasionally seen – a huge, bearded figure pacing the attic room of Glamis castle shouting and waving at an invisible person.

But what of the silver chalice? It still remains at Glamis castle, though maybe if it were returned to its rightful home the curse of the castle would be over, and Patrick would be released from his torment forever. That is something that we'll never know . . .

THE CLAW

The rather crabby monster!

The Kingdom of Dyfed in Wales had been ruled for many years by a Prince who was both just and loved by his people. He was Prince Pwyll, and he ruled with his wife Rhiannon. One fine May-eve Rhiannon gave birth to a son. Six of her ladies-in-waiting sat by the child as she slept, but they soon found their eyelids became strangely heavy, and it wasn't long before they were all asleep. When they woke the boy was gone.

Afraid of what the Prince would say, they lied to Rhiannon, saying that she had killed the child herself. Rhiannon didn't believe her maids, but the rumour spread and she was forced to do penance until news of her son could be found.

Meanwhile, on a near-by estate a Lord named Teyrnon had an exceptionally good mare. Every May-eve this horse would give birth to a foal, but it would always mysteriously disappear. The same year as Rhiannon's baby was born, Teyrnon decided he was going to stay up and discover exactly what happened to his foals.

As usual, the mare had a fine foal. At first everything was still, then suddenly about midnight the silence was broken. Teyrnon saw an enormous claw coming in through the window. It grabbed the foal by the mane, and was lifting it out when Teyrnon struck with his sword. He hit the claw so hard that the monster's arm was cut off. Teyrnon ran outside to follow the creature but the night was dark and it was nowhere to be seen. However, on the ground Teyrnon found a little baby wrapped in silk. He took the child in and Teyrnon and his wife raised him as their own son.

Eventually, the story of Rhiannon's tragedy reached Teyrnon. He immediately realised that the child he had found was her son. So, although it meant grief to Teyrnon and his wife, they decided the child should be returned to its rightful place. The happiness they brought to Pwyll and Rhiannon made it worthwhile. The monster was never seen again, and after that no more children disappeared on May-eve.

KINDNESS CONQUERS ALL!

A leprechaun for luck

Once upon a time, there lived in the heart of Donegal, in Ireland, a prince called Hugh. He was a very kind person and had a great love of animals. One thing pained him, however. He had heard tell of a beautiful princess who had been locked away in a great castle surrounded by a lake. The castle was owned by a giant and a wicked witch who had cast spells on the lake, making any rescue impossible. Hugh hoped that one day he might find a way of helping her.

One summer day, Hugh was sitting near a clump of bushes when a tiny bird fell from its nest. He picked it up and put it back with its mother. Suddenly, a tiny man with a bright smile and sparkling eyes stood before him and said, 'For this kindly deed, a word of advice. Go to the lake that surrounds the giant's castle. There you will see a seagull, which you must strike with this feather.' And with that he disappeared.

Hugh needed no more prompting – he packed his things and set off towards the giant's castle. After a few hours he stopped under an oak tree to have a bite to eat. A bat had got entangled in the ivy of the trunk and was obviously in pain. Hugh set about freeing the bat, and no sooner had he done so than the same little man appeared.

'For this kind deed,' he said, 'take this bat's wing. Turn it three times and thick night will fall around you.' Then he vanished.

Hugh continued on his journey and soon became aware of a high, agonised screeching noise. Following the cries, he found a small black cat stuck at the bottom of a well. Climbing down the well, he brought the cat to safety. Then again the leprechaun appeared.

'Take this cat's eye and all will become light.'

Armed with all these things, Hugh eventually reached the lake surrounding the castle. It was a huge and deep lake and Hugh could think of no way to get across, until he spotted a seagull standing eating worms on the shore. Remembering the leprechaun's words, he touched the bird with the feather and was astounded to see it grow so big that Hugh could climb on to its back. And so he crossed the water.

No sooner had he landed than he was met by the monstrous giant and his ugly wife racing towards him down the great stone steps from the castle. Quick as a flash, Hugh turned the bat's wing three times in his hand and immediately darkness fell. The giant and the witch lost their footing and tumbled headlong into the water. They were never seen again.

Using the cat's eye for light, Hugh followed the winding passages through the gruesome castle to where the Princess lay. With the help of the seagull, he took her home, and within months they were married. Hugh never saw the leprechaun again, but his fame as a lover of animals spread far and wide, and no beast ever suffered again in his kingdom.

BEOWOLF THE BEAST SLAYER

A nasty guest for dinner

There was a kingdom in Denmark which lived under a terrible curse for many years. King Hrothgar and his people lived in fear of Grendel – a monster which visited the Palace every night to eat a number of courtiers. Although each local hero tried to rid the kingdom of the beast, they all suffered the same fate – and provided one more meal for Grendel.

Then, one day, a tall, elegant war-galley was seen entering the harbour. The local watchman feared invaders had come to pillage and plunder. But when the crew disembarked they did not look like the usual group of revellers. The watchman made his way to greet them and found their leader was Beowolf, the nephew of the neighbouring King. News of the terrible fate that hung over King Hrothgar and his people had reached their Kingdom and Beowolf and his brave army were there to battle Grendel.

The watchman led the group to the palace where Hrothgar and his court were feasting. The old King was pleased to see Beowolf, but before allowing him to face Grendel, he warned him of the terrible fate that had come to those who went before him. But Beowolf was not to be put off, so Hrothgar provided him and his men with a great feast and they sat waiting for Grendel to appear.

Night fell and all was peaceful. Then, suddenly the peace was shattered. Grendel came to the door of the hall – for once it was locked and bolted. He was outraged – how dare they try to keep him out?

Using very little effort, Grendel pushed in the door and as it crashed to the floor, Beowolf and his warriors jumped to attention, armed and ready to attack. But Grendel was strong and quick and before anyone could do anything he'd grabbed one of the warriors and gobbled him up. As Grendel reached for another man, Beowolf himself launched his attack. He grabbed Grendel and for the first time Grendel felt real fear as he recognised a strength equal to his own.

Beowolf and Grendel fought, man to beast. Grendel panicked – he forgot about hunting his dinner and thought only to escape – but Beowolf would not let go. Finally, with one last pull, Grendel dragged himself free. But Beowolf's grip was so strong that although he got away Grendel left his arm behind.

Beowolf collapsed, exhausted by his fight, but could be sure that with such a great wound Grendel would certainly die. Some of King Hrothgar's own warriors followed Grendel to make sure that he was dead. Meanwhile the king himself held a great feast to celebrate his kingdom's freedom and Beowolf was the guest of honour.

NARCISSUS & ECHO

Heard it all before!

In the days when the Greek gods ruled the planet, a beautiful child called Narcissus, was born in the island of Thespas. He was the son of the River-god, Cephisus, and was promised to live to a ripe old age, provided he never saw himself. As a child, he was the most attractive boy in the world, and by the time he was sixteen, he had a line of broken-hearted girls in his past.

Meanwhile, another beauty called Echo, had been born. She was a nymph, a kind of half-human, half-spirit, who, at the age of fourteen had upset Hera the wife of the King Zeus. Echo was punished because she lied to Hera. Hera had taken away her power of speech, allowing her only to repeat the last few words of a sentence that someone else might say to her. As if that was not bad enough, Echo had now fallen in love with Narcissus.

One day, Narcissus had got lost in the woods and Echo, who had only stared at him from a distance, wanted to help him, and possibly meet him face to face.

'Is anybody here?' shouted Narcissus.

'Here?' said Echo.

'Come out! Come to me!' said Narcissus.

'Come to me!' said Echo.

'Let us come together!' said Narcissus.

'Come together!' said Echo.

With that, she came out into the open, whereupon the beautiful but vain Narcissus cried out, 'Go away! I hate you!'

This so upset Echo, that she hid in the corner of the woods, and pined away until all that remained of her was her voice.

The gods, meanwhile, were upset with Narcissus for his vain and cruel ways – this was not the first girl who had pined away for him, so they cast a spell which made him fall in love with the next person that he saw, after he woke up from his sleep in the woods. They wanted to make sure that whoever it was, his love would not be returned, so Narcissus would have a taste of his own medicine. As luck would have it, he awoke to see his own image reflected in a silver-clear stream, and fell hopelessly in love with it.

The more he reached for the image in the water, the worse he became, though he soon realised that it was his own self he was gazing at. Thinking that there could be no-one better in the world for him, he pined away too, on that spot by the stream.

Meanwhile, the spirit of Echo, who still followed Narcissus around, grieved for him, and was transformed by the gods into a weeping willow tree by the stream. They transformed Narcissus too, into the white flower of the same name.

Legend has it that whenever you enter a woody glade and see a stream, you'll always see a weeping willow, and the white flower Narcissus. And if you shout out a few words, you'll hear Echo reply – if you listen carefully.

A LOVE THAT REFUSED TO DIE

So true, so faithful, so what?

Many years ago, there was a farmer living in Suffolk. He had only one child, a daughter called Emma. Emma's father had great ambitions for his daughter. He wanted her to marry an aristocrat. But, when she was just eighteen, Emma fell in love with Jethro. He was a worker on her father's land. Emma's father was appalled at the love-match, and refused to let them marry. Instead he banished her, and she was sent to live with an elderly aunt. Jethro was fired.

As he was very poor, Jethro got a job in the only place he could – in a work house. It was full of disease, and before long he caught small-pox and died. Emma's father knew, but he never wrote to tell her, and although he missed her very much he refused to swallow his pride and ask her home.

Meanwhile, Emma was very unhappy. She longed to return home as she missed both her father and Jethro, whom she still believed to be alive. Then one cold winter evening there was a knock at the door. Emma opened it, and there was Jethro.

'I've come to take you home. Your father has forgiven you, and has lent me his best horse so that I can come and collect you. Quick fetch your scarf and we'll go.'

They started their journey. It seemed to Emma as if the horse was galloping incredibly fast. At one point she reached up to touch Jethro's cheek – but withdrew her hand quickly because it was so cold. She took her scarf from around her neck and wrapped it round him.

More quickly than she had realised

possible, they reached home. Jethro told her to go in and wake her father while he put the horse away. Her father was thrilled to see her, and immediately forgot why they had been apart. But he was bemused by the tale Emma told as to how she had got home.

When he went out to the stables there was no sign of anyone, but his horse was sweating, as if it had been on a long journey. He decided that Emma should be told the truth – that Jethro was dead. But Emma did not believe him, and insisted that she should be allowed to see his body.

The next day Emma's father took her to the small grave yard where Jethro was buried.

The grave was opened up and there was Jethro's body – but around his neck was Emma's scarf.

ATLANTIS

Under the sea they are waiting still

Somewhere under the Atlantic ocean lies the lost island city of Atlantis – or so the legend goes. In its day the city ruled a vast empire, while on the island itself there were great gold palaces, luxurious bath houses and herds of elephants were said to roam the mountainous countryside. The Atlantean people were more advanced than any other of this time. They had complicated canal systems and huge trading fleets, which is incredible considering it was more than 3,000 years ago.

Then suddenly, disaster struck. In the space of a day and a night, Atlantis disappeared, without trace. We have no records of where it was or even what happened, only what has been passed down in stories – that some vast natural disaster caused its destruction. Some people have it that Atlantis never existed at all! Others say that the people of Atlantis continued to live under the sea growing webbed feet and coming up only occasionally for air.

There is a theory that Atlantis was none other than the great Minoan civilisation of Crete – and that the legend of the city was based on the volcanic island of Thera, which lies some 120 kms from Crete. Now it consists of three small pieces of land surrounding a huge volcanic crater, which was caused by the volcano collapsing, and the sea rushing in, which resulted in massive explosions, tidal waves and earthquakes. The effect on nearby Crete was disastrous – temples, houses and fleets of ships were destroyed and so was a whole civilisation.

All this ties in very neatly with the

story of Atlantis but there are some flaws in the account. The timing is wrong, for a start, and Crete is certainly not in the Atlantic, the ocean after which Atlantis took its name. Of course the actual ruins never have been found to this very day. Maybe somewhere, sleeping on the sea bed lie the lost people of Atlantis . . . waiting to give us a wave!

FRIEND OR FAWN!

A dear friend or a friendly deer?

The Irish hero Finn was once out hunting with his men and dogs. They had come upon the trail of a fawn which was proving hard to track down. Eventually, only Finn and his two favourite dogs, Bran and Sceolan kept up the hunt. Then, suddenly, Finn was amazed to see the fawn stop in a clearing and turn to greet his dogs. They did not attack her, but immediately made friends. Finn could not believe it. He did not have the heart to kill the fawn so he turned and headed homewards. His dogs and the fawn followed.

That night a beautiful woman appeared before Finn. Her name was Sadbh and she had previously been the fawn. A curse had been put upon her by Dorich the Dark Druid of the men of Dea because she had not returned his love. It could only be broken if Sadbh found herself safe within Finn's own Kingdom. Finn then fell in love with Sadbh and married her. Soon his kingdom was once more at war and Finn led his men out to battle. On his return he went at once to visit Sadbh but she was nowhere to be found.

He searched and searched and eventually came upon a servant who'd seen Sabdh leave the Castle to greet Finn himself. A shadow of Finn with his two dogs had appeared outside the castle, and although the servant had tried to stop her, Sadbh had been determined to greet her husband, the father of the child she was carrying. As soon as she reached the shadow, it transformed into an ugly grey man, and immediately Sadbh was once more turned into a fawn. She'd tried desperately to return to the castle, but the two fierce dogs had stopped her and she was dragged away.

Finn spent the next seven years in torment searching for his wife, but he found no sign of her. Until one day when he was again out hunting. His dogs came upon a small boy. It was obvious that the boy could communicate with dogs like an animal. He was more nervous of Finn and his men. Finn saw the boy was very beautiful and intelligent looking, and that perhaps in his face there was a shadow of his wife Sadbh. Thinking that this might be his son he took the boy home with him. The boy was indeed his own son. He had been looked after by the fawn until the ugly grey man had taken her away. Finn named the boy Oisin, and he grew to become a great Irish poet and hero.

ELDORADO

Greed for gold gets dampened down!

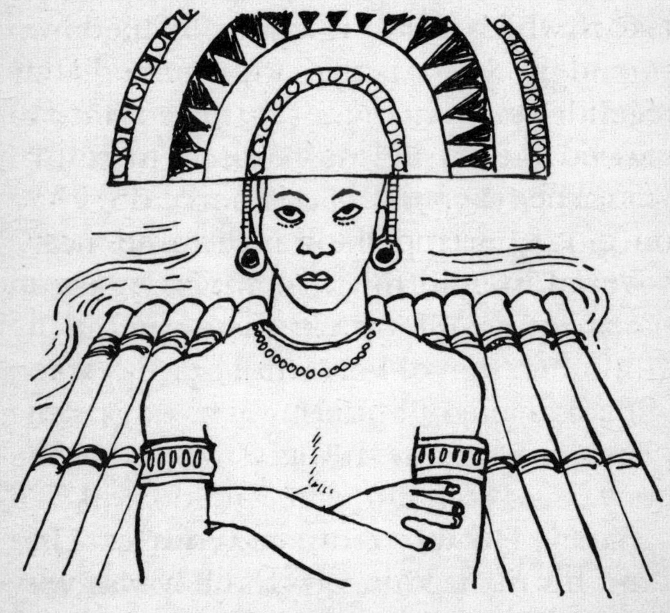

For the past 400 years and more explorers have searched for Eldorado – a place that is supposed to contain wealth beyond the bounds of imagination. It all started when the Spaniards invaded South America in the 16th century. There they found more gold and precious stones than they had ever seen. They killed the native people and their chiefs, and set to stripping their temples and homes of all the riches they could find. But they were greedy for more. In the heart of the Andes there was a deep lake in which it was rumoured millions of pounds worth of gold were sunk. The legend ran that there was a ceremony carried out by a local tribe. The chief would be taken to the middle of the lake on a raft, stripped of his clothes and covered in gold dust. At the same time the tribes-people would throw pieces of gold into the lake. Eldorado does mean gilded one in Spanish and it seems probable that this is where the story was born.

And so the expeditions started. In 1545 the Spaniards forced the tribesmen to form a human chain from the lake to the mountain tops and attempt to empty the lake with buckets. Since then several channels have been built to drain the water, and although bits and pieces of gold and emeralds have been found, they have never successfully drained the lake to find the promised hoards of treasure. Even 20th century drilling proved useless.

Now the site is protected, so it looks as though the treasures will remain undisturbed. But some people say that the ceremonies still happen, and that in other parts of the Andes, tribe leaders continue to be showered with gold as part of their inauguration ceremony. The spirit of Eldorado still lives on . . .

STONEHENGE

The original rock opera!

In the middle of Salisbury Plain stands the huge stone circle of Stonehenge. But how old are the boulders, and who built them into strange shapes? And why, on Midsummer's morning, do druids meet at the stone for ancient rituals?

The first puzzle is how forty- or fifty-ton rocks were moved and shaped to make the circle. One story says that a race of giants brought them from Africa to Ireland, while another legend says that the wizard Merlin enlisted the help of the Devil to fly them over to Salisbury Plain. In truth, it seems most likely that they were moved (using rafts and rollers) over two hundred miles from the mountains of South Wales.

It is hard to guess how old the temple really is. Archaeologists think it was built in three stages over a space of five hundred years. The first builders lived in the late Stone Age – some four thousand years ago. But why would people make such a superhuman effort just to build a stone circle? Some say that it was a centre for human sacrifice – ancient skulls have been found near one of the stones called the Slaughter Stone. Others say that the stones are arranged to be a prehistoric computer which can work out the movement of the planets and stars. But many people see Stonehenge as a huge shrine dedicated to worshipping the sun. Golden sun discs have been found in nearby graves. Druids have flocked to Stonehenge for thousands of years (modern-day druids still go there now) to witness an event which gives weight to the theory that the circle was a centre of sun worship. As the sun comes up on Midsummer morning, it can be seen to rise precisely through the centre of the temple's entrance. But whatever the history of Stonehenge is, its strangely angled stones hold secrets and mysteries that will never be revealed.

DON'T DALLY WITH A DEMON!

Don't sleep with your mouth open

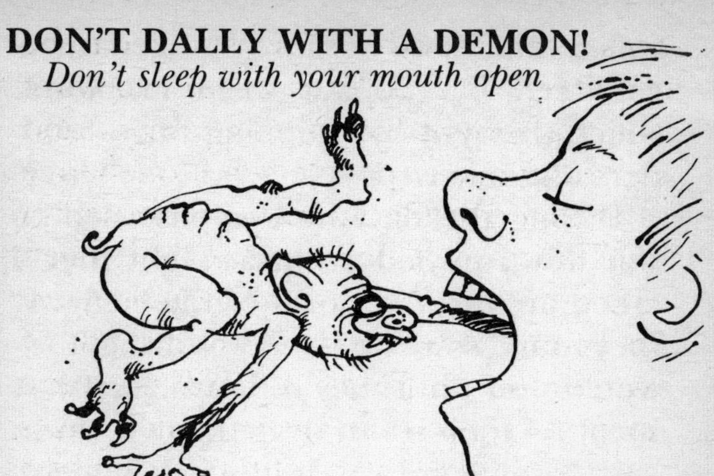

Of all the nasty, disgusting, horrible creatures that lived in the world of the supernatural, the most repulsive were the demons. They were blamed for everything. If a person was ill, if someone was a bit mad, everyone would say, 'Aaahh! – they've got a demon inside them!' Some people said the demons were angels who'd been sent down to hell for rebelling against God; others said they were spirits who floated through the air trying to destroy everything in the world that was good. There was one called 'Corpse Tearer'; another called 'Eurynome' (who ate human flesh); and the Scottish Demons were called 'Red Caps' because they kept their caps red by dipping them in blood, which they got by dropping huge boulders on their victims.

During the day the demons used to stay down in hell – but at night they'd creep up into the world of the living. If they found someone who was dying, they would wait until they'd drawn their last breath – then try to drag them down to hell. If someone was desperately in debt, the demons would offer to pay their bills provided they promised to give themselves to the devil when they died. To make sure, they would get them to sign a contract in their own blood.

But above all, you had to make sure that you didn't yawn – because if you did, a demon would jump down your throat and make you one of the Devil's slaves.

Nowadays, not many people believe in demons, so most of them stay down in hell, keeping themselves warm by their fires. But they do come out occasionally, so whatever you do, everytime you yawn, make sure you put your hand over your mouth – otherwise . . . Aaaagghh!!!

POLTERGEISTS

And finally – an explanation for almost anything!

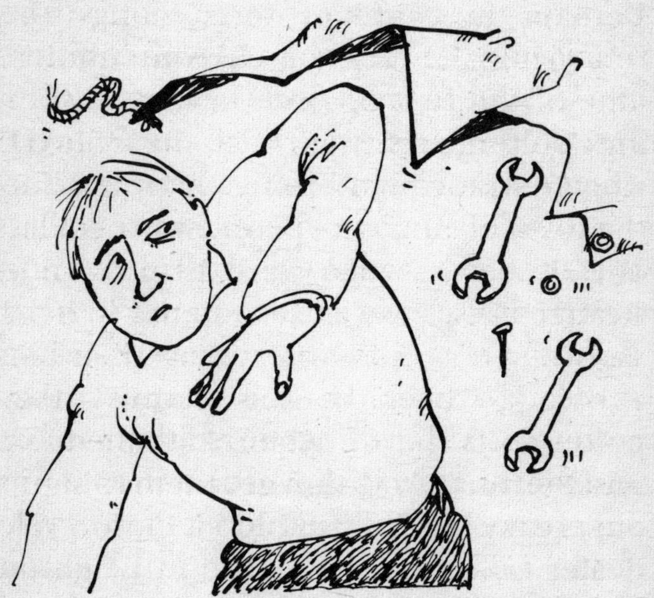

You've all heard the phrase, 'ghosties and ghoulies and things that go bump in the night'. Well, the ghosties and ghoulies are usually whispy white forms that walk through walls, without making any noise, so who – or what – makes things go bump in the night?

Many people believe that poltergeists are responsible. Their favourite tricks are knocking on walls, throwing cups and moving furniture – a bit like supernatural removal men! The word poltergeist is German (it means 'noisy spirit'). Perhaps the Germans were amongst the first victims of these mischievous ghouls. One of the first recorded events involving poltergeists was back in 355AD, when extraordinary things happened to the town of Bingen – people were pulled out of bed, stones were thrown, and strange noises were heard in the dead of night.

But it's been in this century that poltergeists have been at their most mischievous. And they don't just haunt old creaky houses! In 1963 a motorcycle dealer called Sid, who lived in Leighton Buzzard, decided to knock down a wall in his workshop. The day after the demolition, Sid found three of his motorbikes mysteriously damaged, and thrown on to the floor. Vandals? Sid thought little of it until the next day. He was in his workshop when suddenly he saw his neatly placed spanners fly off their hooks. Then, behind him, a tarpaulin flew into the air, like a huge bird! No one has ever been able to explain the problems that Sid had – perhaps the poltergeist was a budding bike mender!

But the most famous poltergeist case of all happened on the island of Barbados, at the site of a stone-built tomb. For many years it contained only one coffin, Mrs Thomasina Goddard's. In 1808, a new family put the coffins of their two daughters in the tomb which was re-sealed when they left. A few years later, when the tomb was re-opened to bury another member of the family, the mourners were astonished to find that the coffins of the two girls had been pushed right against the end of the tomb – and Mrs Goddard's coffin hadn't been touched. This happened several times and each time there had been no sign of thieves breaking into the tomb. Not that anyone would try to move the coffins unless they had to – it normally took eight men to pick them up because they were made of lead.

Finally, the governor took a hand. He opened the tomb and sprinkled sand on all the coffins, then re-sealed the tomb tightly. Then he chose a day at random, turned up unexpectedly and asked to look inside the tomb again. A chilling sight faced him. All but one of the heavy coffins had been stacked upright in one corner. Mrs Goddard's coffin still lay in the middle of the floor with the sand on it untouched. That was enough for the governor and the family. All the other coffins were moved and buried underground. The strange poltergeist who lived in the tomb never emerged again.

So, the next time your homework mysteriously disappears from your desk, try telling the teacher a poltergeist took it – it's a better excuse than 'the dog ate it'!